Tying Saltwater Flies
12 of the Best

Deke Meyer

GUIDO RAHR

Frank Amato
PORTLAND

Welcome To Tying Saltwater Flies

Through step-by-step photos and description this book will show you how to tie the dozen best saltwater flies. By varying the size and color of the given patterns, you can catch most species of fish that swim the seas. Of course, it's impossible to include all the world's excellent saltwater patterns, so these flies were chosen to represent 12 different fly *designs*, and at the same time, keeping them simple enough for the beginning tier. Each fly is designed to perform in a specific way, to mimic prey fish or simulate a crustacean or just appeal to larger predator gamefish.

Besides offering 12 flies that catch fish and 12 styles of flies, this book presents varied fly tying techniques, including traditional approaches and some new ones that use epoxy, silicone and hot glue.

This dozen of saltwater's finest flies have proven themselves as effective fish catchers because they not only trigger saltwater fish to strike, but they also offer minimum air resistance when cast and hold up to the rigors of saltwater fly fishing. Their originators designed these flies to be slim enough to cast well, but with the durability needed to withstand sharp fish teeth and rigorous casting.

Tying Saltwater Flies attempts to give you all the information you need to tie these flies, but it can be very helpful if you watch a friend, fly club member, or a fly shop person tie these flies.

GUIDO RAHR

Published in 1996 by Frank Amato Publications, Inc.
P.O. Box 82112, Portland, Oregon 97282

All photographs taken by the author except where noted.
Cover photograph: Jim Schollmeyer   Back cover photograph: Frank Amato
Book design and layout: Tony Amato

Softbound ISBN: 1-57188-066-6   UPC: 0-66066-00257-0
Printed in Hong Kong

1 3 5 7 9 10 8 6 4 2

TABLE OF CONTENTS

Shopping for Tools and Materials

A supportive local fly club or fly shop is ideal and can prove to be a wealth of information. Mail order is workable if you get a knowledgeable salesperson via a 1-800 number.

Shopping for a Vise

You need a fly tying vise, which range in price from inexpensive to very expensive, depending on workmanship and quality of the metals used. If you're on a budget, I recommend buying an inexpensive vise at first, then as you gain experience you will define your own preferences. Later on you can get a vise that will last a lifetime. You can use your first vise as a field kit vise or pass it on to another beginning tier.

For tying saltwater flies, it's important that the vise can clamp down tightly on the larger hooks that saltwater flies demand—if the hook slips, you'll just frustrate yourself and you won't be able to tie the fly. (If you're at a fly shop, have the sales clerk clamp a 1/0 saltwater hook in the vise, then you can pull on it to see if it holds tight.)

You might want to consider a rotating vise, which will aid you in tying: you can rotate the fly while it's still in the vise so you can view the fly from all sides as you tie it; you can turn the fly while in the vise to tie materials to the underside of the fly. (If you apply epoxy, hot glue or silicone to the fly while it's in the vise, you can rotate the fly so it dries evenly.)

You will need a pair of heavy duty scissors, bobbin, bobbin threader and whip finish tool. Be sure to get scissors with finger holes that fit properly. Many are too small. Unlike tying trout flies, which often demands scissors with fine points for delicate work, for saltwater flies you need heavy duty scissors that can repeatedly cut coarse materials. When buying scissors, specify that you plan to tie saltwater flies.

Saltwater Hooks

The most important component in fly tying is the hook. For resistance to salt corrosion, you will need either stainless steel hooks or those plated in nickel or other corrosion resistant material. You can tie and fish with inexpensive hooks but you will miss catching fish because the steel is too soft and the hook is usually dull.

I recommend paying a little more and getting the best hook you can buy. After all, when you consider the amount of time and money you

spend on tying flies, and your investment in fly fishing gear, then driving, boating or flying to the fishing area, why scrimp a few cents on a hook?

For years, the traditional saltwater hook has been the Mustad 34007. But when shopping for hooks, bear in mind that there is no standard size or nomenclature in the industry. Consequently, I refer to hooks as standard (as compared to the 34007) or extra long or extra short, etc.

Hook quality has changed dramatically in recent years, with manufacturers offering super-sharp hooks of high quality. Newer versions of the Mustad 34007 are now offered by Mustad, Daiichi, Eagle Claw, Gamakatsu, Tiemco and VMC.

Synthetics

In recent years, the most profound influence on saltwater flies is the overwhelming use of iridescent plastics in wing, tail and body materials. You will encounter a staggering variety of brand names for comparable types of materials. In some cases the synthetics are so similar as to be interchangeable; in other instances the materials are varied enough to exhibit different properties which can affect tying and fishing the fly. I've mentioned some specific names, but the market changes fast, so knowledgeable sales people can offer valuable help.

How to Proceed— Tying the First Flies

There is a tremendous variety of fish to catch in the salt, so once you determine what you hope to catch, then you can pick the appropriate hook sizes. For example, for smaller inshore fish you might go with size 2 or 4; bigger inshore species, 1 and 1/0; for bonefish you might add size 6 and 8; for tarpon, 2/0 and 3/0. It can be confusing at first, so don't be afraid to ask fly fishing salespeople to help you out. You can buy hooks in boxes of 100 or in packages of 25. You may want to get the smaller packets first, so you can have a range of sizes. Also, you will eventually want to add bendback hooks and extra short and extra long shank hooks, as well.

Thread is inexpensive: start with size A or 3/0 flat waxed fly tying thread in white, then add some bright colors such as orange and red and neutral colors such as tan, gray or pale olive.

In lieu of collecting your own materials, you may wish to use a pre-assembled kit, such as the

Basic Tools

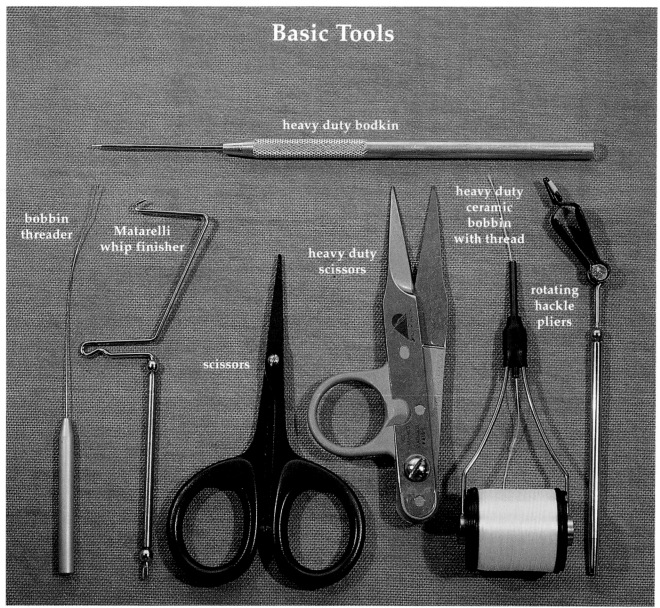

Besides a vise, basic tools needed for tying include: (from the left) bobbin threader, Matarelli whip finisher (Extended Reach recommended), scissors, heavy duty scissors, heavy duty ceramic bobbin with thread, rotating hackle pliers and (on top) heavy duty bodkin.

Dupli-Kits offered by Umpqua Feather Merchants. These include kits for tying the Crazy Charlie, Clouser Minnow, Popovics Banger and Lefty's Deceiver.

Before tying, mash the barb down on the hook with pliers. (If you accidentally break the hook, you won't forfeit an already tied fly.) Most of us practice catch-and-release fly fishing with barb-less hooks, but just as important, if you stick your clothes or your anatomy with a hook, it will easily come out. Always wear some kind of eye protection—you can lose your sight to a fly hook.

It might seem complicated at first glance, but fly tying is simply a matter of practice and proportion. My first flies looked as if they had ejected from the vacuum cleaner, only to be stomped by indifferent feet. But I caught fish with those unruly flies. With practice comes improvement, and fish eat imperfect flies.

I wish you enjoyable tying and fishing.

Recommended Video

"POP FLEYES", saltwater patterns tied by Bob Popovics (Umpqua Feather Merchants, 1995)

Attaching The Thread To The Hook

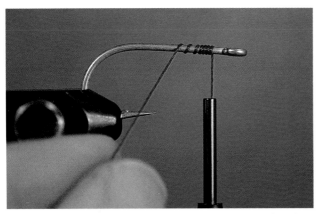

1) Hold end of thread between thumb and forefinger of left hand, wrap thread around hook shank with thread bobbin in right hand.

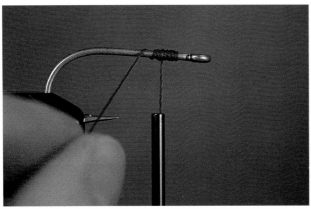

2) While maintaining light pressure on thread with thumb and forefinger of left hand, wrap thread back over itself with bobbin.

Drying Flies

For drying flies, a rotating tool works well, slowly turning the flies so they dry evenly. (Courtesy of The Fly Shop, 1-800-669-FISH)

The Whip Finish

Using a Matarelli whip finish tool is highly recommended because it is quick and easy to use once you learn how, and the head on the fly will be small and tight, making your fly more durable. (For saltwater flies, the Matarelli Extended Reach whip finish tool recommended.)

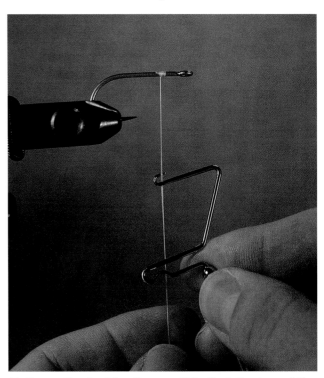

1) Grasp the tool by the small ball at the top of the handle between thumb and forefinger of right hand, thread bobbin in left hand. Tool hook goes around thread; bottom bend stays on your side.

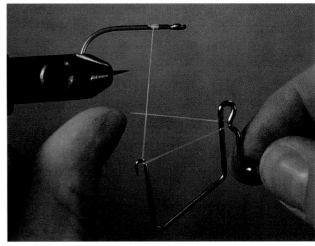

2) Allow tool to pivot on ball between thumb and forefinger: thread forms triangle, from head of fly, through tool hook, around tool bend, then back across in front of thread from head of fly.

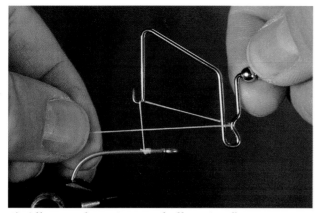

3) Allow tool to pivot on ball again, flipping triangle upside down and bringing triangle above hook, maintaining light pressure on thread bobbin. (The tool bend stays on the right side while the tool hook flips out towards you, ending above the hook shank, but still in a triangle.)

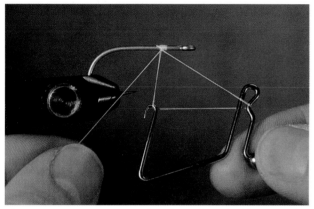

4) Keeping tension on the thread and allowing the tool to pivot on the ball, keep the tool bend to the right and wrap thread around the hook shank with the tool hook three times. (You still have the triangle, the tool hook flips out towards you while the tool bend stays to the right.)

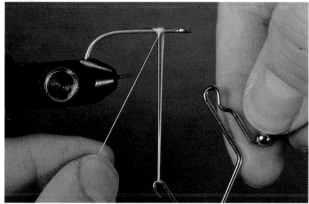

5) Maintain pressure on the thread and on the tool hook, tip the tool bend down until the thread slips off, leaving thread attached to the head of the fly and the tool hook.

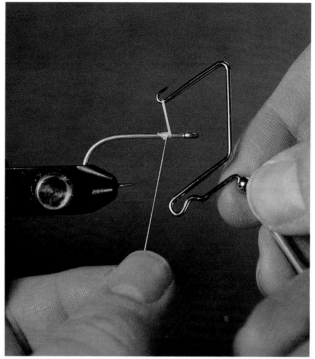

6) Pull on the thread while sliding the tool hook up to the fly head.

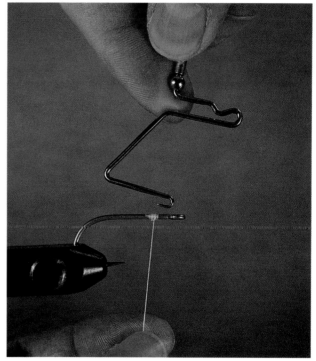

7) Tip the tool hook until the thread slips off, tightening the thread, which finishes the whip finish. (Instead of wrapping thread around the fly head six times (Step 4) it's better to make two complete whip finishes of three wraps each. It makes a tighter head and if the first whip finish breaks you still have a usable fly and you can add another whip finish later.)

Apte Tarpon Fly

Apte Tarpon Fly—Stu Apte

Stu told me, "This fly dates back to 1958. I was probably the first to tie the tail way back so it didn't hook-wrap. The early ones were tied with neck hackle and they were quite splayed so they curved outward. Later, in the 1960's, I started using saddle hackle, which swims nicer."

Hook: Eagle Claw L067, 254SS; Tiemco 811S; sizes 2/0 to 4/0
Thread: Orange (exposed front thread covered with epoxy)
Tail: Saddle hackle, splayed out, orange in the middle of two yellow hackle on each side
Hackle: Palmered, yellow and orange, two or three saddle hackles
Tailguard: Loop of stiff 15-pound monofilament (Mason hard monofilament)

substitutes a rabbit strip for the hackle tail. Apte has taken 19 tarpon over 150 pounds and six world record tarpon on these flies.

Stu says, "This fly doesn't look like much when you hold it in your hand, but when you put it in the water, it looks like a Super Dude, which is the name I originally came up with in 1979. I fished it in the Keys and did really well with it—fish just jumped all over it—better than anything else I'd ever used.

"When Ralph Delph saw it in the water, he said, *Hey, what do you call that thing—it really looks good.* I said, well, I call it a Super Dude. He says, *No, any fish that sees that is apt to eat it—you have to call it the Apte Too.*"

Tying Tips

Stu says, "The best thing is to have good material. Nothing surpasses having good material to work with. It's really important that the tail feathers have to be the same length." He says the width isn't as important. When he palmers on the body hackle, he wraps all of them at the same time. He says, "I think you'll find it pretty easy, especially if you have a fairly limber feather." A beginner can certainly wrap them one at a time, especially if the stems are stiff and unwieldy.

For the anti-fouling tailguard, Stu says, "I use a piece of 15-pound hard mono and make a loop that extends back there beyond the hook. As a matter of fact, that's not my idea—I got it from Steve Rajeff. Steve and I were sitting at my house in the Keys and tying flies, and that was the first time I'd ever seen that."

Stu recommends putting epoxy on the thread. He says, "Tarpon, snook, a lot of these fish have a very rough mouth and if you don't do that, you get one hit or a second hit, and the threads start unraveling."

Variations

Stu says, "The orange and yellow color combination is only one of six different colors that I tie, including yellow and white, black and red, and black and yellow."

The Apte Too has a squirrel tail collar and tail hackles that come together and don't splay. The Apte Too Plus

Fishing Stories

Stu says, "This past May I know that I cast to some fish down in the lower Keys that I cast to, in the same exact place, 30-odd years before. I mean, it was exactly the same fish that I fished before. Tarpon live a long time. Some of those fish were 130 pounds or so, in the 1960's, and they are 170 to 180 now. They live a long, long time. They were probably 30-odd or 40-odd years old then. Now they're 60 or 70 years old. Scientists tell us that a tarpon that weighs 180 pounds is probably 70 years old. They're prehistoric, you know. Tarpon were around in the dinosaur days.

"I had a customer, back in the early days, that hooked the biggest tarpon that I've ever seen. It was closer to 300 than 250. That was in 1963 or 1964. It was over eight feet long, and it was so big around it was grotesque. The guy broke it off on the first jump. He went through 22 fish that day and never had one on for more than one jump."

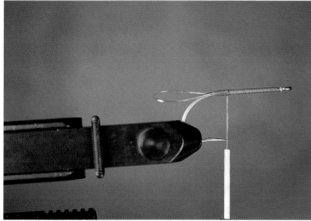

1) Debarb hook. Attach thread rear of hook, wrap thread to front and back to rear. Tie in loop of 15-pound hard monofilament (extends 1/2 hook shank length to rear, parallel to shank). Trim excess and cement.

2) Select six saddle hackles, matching two pair of three so ends are even (yellow-orange-yellow). If they curve, match them to curve to outside. Tie in first three on far side (extending about 1 1/2 hook shank length to rear), parallel to hook shank. Leave stubs (see 4b) for better tie-in but don't crimp stem.

3) Tie in other three on this side. Trim excess and cement. (Vise rotated for photo.)

4) Tie in three saddle hackles (yellow-orange-yellow) so they curve to rear—shiny side forward, width about hook gap or a little wider. (Measure hackle width and clip it where stem gets thin.)
4b insert) Leave short hackle fiber stubs for better grip by thread. Crimp stem with thumbnail so hackle wraps at right angle to shank.

5) Wrap hackle around hook shank (either all three at once or as singles; hackle pliers are helpful). Tie off and trim excess, cement tie-down spot.

6) Wrap thread to eye. Whip finish and cement. Cover thread with thin coat of 5-minute epoxy.

Bendback

Bendback

Hook: Bendback Mustad 34005; Tiemco 411S; Mustad keel hook 79666S; varied sizes
Tail: Optional, usually not included
Gills: Optional, red thread, paint or permanent marker
Wing: Bucktail or synthetics; Krystal Flash or Flashabou; optional grizzly hackle, peacock herl topping
Body: Tubular mylar, braided poly flash or chenille
Eyes: Optional, painted or adhesive
Options: Lead wire on shank
Variations: Numerous, including all white, yellow, chartreuse, purple, black, green/white, blue/white, red/white, red/yellow, orange/yellow; enclosed rattle

The Bendback is a generalist baitfish imitation originally tied on a Mustad 34007 hook, with the hook shank bent with a pair of pliers to change the hook configuration to lessen snag-ups. Although you can still do that, Mustad's 34005 is the bendback style of the 34007; and Tiemco offers the chemically sharpened 411S bendback. A different design, the Mustad keel style 79666S in stainless steel is made with softer wire and a longer hook shank (the Mustad 34005 in size 1 is equivalent to a size 6 keel).

Tying Tips

The idea behind the bendback style is to lessen snag-ups by guarding the hook point with the wing, but also to retrieve the fly in a hook-up position. You can enhance that hook-up strategy by adding lead wire to the rear half of the hook shank, either by wrapping lead around it, much like you wrap thread, or by lashing a strip of lead wire parallel to the shank.

Variations

You can tie the body by wrapping braided poly flash around the hook shank as illustrated, or slip a tubular material such as mylar tubing over the shank. Attach the thread to the rear of the body, slip the tubing over the shank, then tie off the rear end of the tubing with a whip finish, snip the thread and apply cement. (As a variation, you can tease out strands of the material, forming a sparkle tail.) You then cut the tubing at the front end of the body, re-attach the thread, and then tie down the end of the tubing, securing it to the hook shank. Depending on its diameter, you may need to wrap an underbody to pump out the tubing properly and to prevent the tubing from excessively fraying when you fish the fly.

An interesting variation is to add a rattle under the body material (usually under tubing). These rattles are two or three BB's enclosed in a sealed tube of either plastic or aluminum. The clicking of the rattle is thought to mimic sounds made by the gills of panicked baitfish or by predator gamefish just prior to their feeding charge. In any case, the clacking of the rattle draws fish to the strike and can be an advantage, particularly when water clarity is less than ideal.

Wing materials vary, including bucktail or synthetics such as FisHair, Super Hair and Ultra Hair. You can add sparkle with Flashabou or Krystal Flash, in any number of color combinations. The challenge with the Bendback is tying the wings in while the hook is upside down, and in a small tie-down area.

Adding eyes endows a lifelike aspect to the fly as a baitfish simulation, particularly in clear water. Even in murky water, when the gamefish closes in on the fly, the eye may be the final trigger to trip the predator into striking your fly. First, make your head wraps smooth, avoiding lumps, and then give the head at least two coats of head cement to form a smooth base for the eyes. You can paint on a yellow, red or white eye and then a black pupil, or paint a black pupil on a colored thread head. You can use a miniature brush, or wooden dowel or round toothpick (trimmed with a razor blade) of two different sizes. The easiest way is to apply an adhesive eye (just peel off the backing and place the eye on the fly). With either method, you can protect the eye by applying a finish coat of water-based clear enamel fixative (found at craft stores) or 5-minute epoxy.

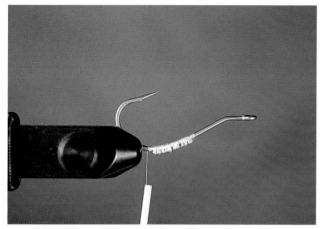

1) Debarb hook. Insert (bendback) hook in vise, inverted, attach thread. Tie in lead wire parallel to the shank, covering the rear 1/2 of the shank. Cement thread wraps.

2) Tie in body material (laid along shank from rear to wing tie-down area; leave room to tie in wing). Bring thread to front of body.

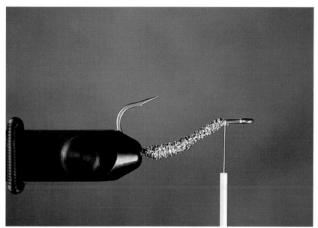

3) Wrap body to wing tie-in area, tie off and trim excess (leave room to tie in wing).

4) Tie in wing materials and trim. (Wing extends back about hook shank length.)

5) With thread build head big enough for eyes. Whip finish and trim. Apply head cement.

6) Apply second coat of head cement (allow the first to dry). (Add gills with red paint or marker.) Apply paint for eyes or attach adhesive eyes, then a coat of fixative or epoxy (if eyes painted, allow to dry before applying fixative).

Bob's Banger

Bob's Banger—Bob Popovics

Hook: Extra long shank, non-kinked: Mustad 92611;
    Eagle Claw 66SS; size 2/0
Thread: Size D or C rod wrapping thread, any color
Tail: Bucktail, varied colors
Body: Plastic chenille; Livebody foam; prismatic tape,
    varied colors
Eyes: Adhesive prismatic 3/8 inch

The Bob Popovics video "Pop Fleyes" is highly recommended; one of the flies he ties is a Banger, and he gives some tips about fishing Bangers. You might consider the Popovics' Banger Dupli-Kit by Umpqua, which contains enough material to tie 12 poppers in three colors.

(The Mustad 92608 in stainless steel mentioned in the video has been discontinued, replaced by the Mustad 92611 in nickel. The chemically sharpened Mustad 34039SS in stainless steel size 2/0 is only a bit shorter, and a good bet.)

The rationale behind his Banger series is twofold: quick and easy to tie poppers; and interchangeable heads for changing fishing conditions. As Bob says in his video, he can tie a whole season's worth of Bangers in one evening, as opposed to spending several weeks tying traditional poppers. And when the calm morning's fishing is superseded by wind, you can quickly replace the popper head with a smaller one.

Tying Tips

Bob uses rod wrapping thread so he can quickly cover the long shank with thread, and the bulkier thread binds the foam head solidly to the hook.

To bore the hole in the foam, Bob uses a large diameter bodkin that he heats with a lighter. You might also try a smaller bodkin (or needle clamped with locking pliers) to make a pilot hole, then enlarge the hole with a drill bit (twisted by hand or held by pliers). The hole should be big enough so the foam can go over the hook eye, but small enough to grip the thread-covered hook shank. Be sure that the hole is centered.

Variations

Color schemes vary, including fluorescent orange, green, yellow and silver. It makes sense to tie poppers in different colors to accomplish the basic idea behind poppers: to attract fish under varied conditions of light and water clarity; and to mimic a maimed baitfish in trouble.

You should vary the diameter of the foam body because you'll fish poppers in varied conditions. You'll have trouble casting a large diameter popper in wind, and in calm, clear conditions you may spook fish instead of attracting them. On the other hand, to stir fish to the strike in turbid water, you may need a big face popper.

1) Debarb hook, attach thread, cover hook shank and cement. Tie in bucktail at rear (extends hook shank length), trim excess and cement.

4) Bore centered hole in foam, large enough to pass over hook eye, but still be tight to hook. Slide foam over hook.

2) Tie in plastic chenille.

5) Wrap on adhesive tape, overlapping for good adherence.

3) Wrap chenille forward, tie off, trim excess (leave 1/2 hook shank for popper head). Whip finish and cement.

6) Attach eyes to foam.

Clouser's Deep Minnow

Clouser's Deep Minnow—Bob Clouser

Hook: Standard length; varied sizes
Thread: White
Tail: Forms lower wing and belly, white bucktail
Wing: Rainbow Krystal Flash; pale gray bucktail
Body: Tying thread over bucktail
Eyes: Weighted: lead, plated or non-toxic
Variations: All black; chartreuse and white; chartreuse and yellow; and red and white. The Skinny Water Clouser Minnows have white Super Hair tails and wings of gray, chartreuse, red or tan.

Bob told me, " The original Deep Minnow was designed for the darting motion of baitfish trying to escape a predator. It gives the look of a baitfish and it's sparsely dressed. The darting motion comes from the stripping, or the motion you give the fly after the cast is done. If you would take an older pattern that has no weight at any definite spot in the fly, and you strip it. The fly stops dead and doesn't move. This creates a wonderment from a predator because all his life, every time he fed on baitfish, he has to catch it to eat it. And it usually scurries and hides somewhere.

"The Deep Minnow—when you stop your retrieve and your stripping—will drop off its plane and head towards the bottom. From either side—it doesn't necessarily drop straight down; it gets off plane and slides off to the side—mimicking that downward movement of a baitfish trying to hide. So that's one of the main effective features of the fly—with lead eyes attached at a 1/3 point in back of the eye—it gives it that motion."

Tying Tips

Because the weighted eyes are tied on top of the hook, the fly swims with the point up, reducing snag-ups. Bob says, "The lead eyes make the fly dip and dart with an action and speed similar to a live baitfish fleeing from a predator."

Bob secures the hair for the belly of this baitfish imitation in front of and in back of the eyes, keeping the belly slender, just like the natural fish. The hair for the top or back of the baitfish is tied only in front of the eyes so that it angles up. And one of the keys to this fly is using only a small batch of hair—keep it sparse. The illusion is further enhanced with sparkle material in the center, adding a bit of light reflecting translucency.

Lefty Kreh and Bob Clouser often fish together and share ideas. Lefty first fished the Clouser Deep Minnow in August of 1988. He wrote, "During the next four months I fished the Deep Minnow in fresh and salt water from the south Pacific to Labrador. During that time I caught 24 species of freshwater and saltwater fish—everything from sharks and bonefish to walleyes and bluegills.

"This fly must be tied sparsely to be effective. If it is constructed with very little material, the Deep Minnow perfectly resembles a minnow in the water. It's transparent—just a little of the back and side can be seen underwater—and the lead eyes are truly visible. The fly also sinks quickly when sparsely dressed. Overdressing spoils the pattern's appearance and its appeal to fish and slows the sink rate. Because the pattern is tied with a reverse-style wing, the hook point rides up and rarely snags on the bottom."

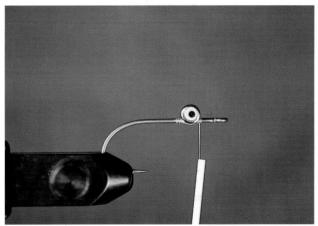

1) Attach thread. Tie in eyes securely, on front 1/3 of hook shank. Make sure eyes are level.

2) Apply one drop of Zap-A-Gap super glue to thread.

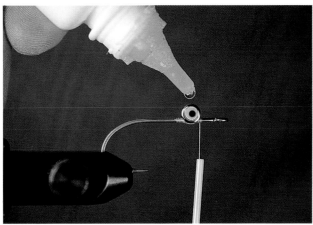

3) Tie in sparse clump of white bucktail, about 20 strands. (Extends to rear about one hook shank length.) First, tie it down in front of eyes, then tie it down behind eyes. Trim excess bucktail. Move thread to front. (Whip finish with two wraps to hold thread in place.)

4) Invert hook in vise (if your vise rotates, then rotate). Tie in 20 strands of rainbow Krystal Flash, in front of eyes only, as a center wing. Trim excess.

5) Tie in sparse clump of gray bucktail, about 20 strands, in front of eyes only. Trim excess.

6) Whip finish and cement thread.

15

Crazy Charlie

Crazy Charlie—Bob Nauheim

Hook: Standard length, sizes 2-8
Thread: White
Tail: Silver Flashabou *[handwritten: crystal flash]*
Body: Silver tinsel; mono or clear V-rib *[handwritten: saua loce (orange)]*
Wing: Cream or white hackle or calf tail *[handwritten: few strands crystal flash]*
Eyes: Silver bead chain
Variations: This is the original pattern; there are countless variations in color and materials; most omit the tail.

Bob told me, "I came up with the original Crazy Charlie on Andros Island in the Bahamas in the late '70's and named it for Bonefish Charlie Smith. I originally tied it to emulate glass minnows but we soon realized that the bonefish were taking it as a shrimp. Originally the fly was called the "Nasty Charlie" because Charlie had said, *"Dat fly nasty!"* when we first took fish on it.

"I took the pattern to Key West and showed it to Capt. Jan Isley, who was then guiding there, and Jan had great success with the pattern on fussy Keys bonefish. Jan was the first to tie the fly with a hair wing. We next took it to Christmas Island when that mid-Pacific atoll first opened to bonefishing. The first fly fishermen who fished the island told us that the bonefish there had refused all of their offerings and they didn't think they would take a fly. Don't forget, this was the first time anyone had ever seriously fished for bonefish in the Pacific with a fly.

"But we were very successful with the Crazy Charlie, and when we got back, Leigh Perkins of Orvis called me. Perkins was planning a trip to the island and wanted the pattern with which we had been so successful. When he returned after a successful trip to Christmas Island he had the fly dressed commercially for Orvis, and inadvertently changed the "Nasty" to "Crazy", hence the Crazy Charlie. The fly marketed through Orvis was a huge success and soon others began tying the pattern commercially. The Crazy Charlie was well on its way to becoming the most popular bonefish pattern ever to come down the pike!"

Variations

The Crazy Charlie is probably the most famous and successful inverted wing bonefish fly of all time, with dozens of variations cropping up in the years since its inception. Some

use synthetic wing and tail material, and there are many colors used in Crazy Charlies, including pink, chartreuse, yellow, orange, and others. Some coat the body with epoxy for increased durability.

It's roots include Pete Perinchief's Horror, of which he says, "It was way back in 1953 or '54 that the Horror was devised. My good and long time friend Joe Brooks, along with myself, gave the Horror a thorough field testing and it worked very well and consistently in the taking of bonefish. Since that time the design has not changed." The Horror is simplicity itself, consisting of an inverted brown bucktail wing mounted 1/4 hook shank length behind the eye, and long enough to extend past the hook, with a dab of yellow chenille in front of the wing, tied down with red thread.

Winston Moore created another pioneering fly, Agent Orange, with an orange chenille body and an inverted wing of orange hair and two grizzly hackle tips. He told me, "Thirty years ago when I first used the fly there weren't that many flies with much color in them. I used to fish it a lot in Belize, in small sizes, in 6's and 8's and it was absolutely deadly. I hooked so many hundreds of bonefish down there on that fly that you wouldn't believe it, on any kind of a bottom, grassy, sand, or mud or whatever. So when I started fishing the Bahamas at Andros Island with Bonefish Charlie, I naturally had some of these with me. He'd never seen it and I'd never fished it in the Bahamas. It was so effective down there; I remember one day he and I were out in his skiff and I was taking fish after fish and he said, *"Mon, you don't need no guide, all you needs is that orange fly."*

Possibly the oldest bonefish fish of this type is the Frankee-Belle Bonefish Fly created just after WWII by Frankee Albright and Belle Mathers, tied with a white chenille body and a brown bucktail wing enclosed with grizzly hackle tips.

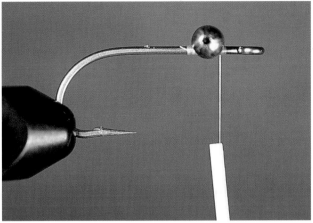

1) Debarb hook, attach thread, tie down eyes on front 1/4 of shank, securely. Make sure eyes level, put one drop Zap-A-Gap super glue on tie-down.

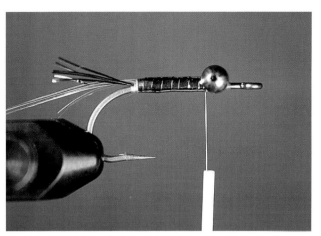

4) Wrap tinsel, tightly, to rear and then forward, over itself, back to behind eyes, tie down and trim excess.

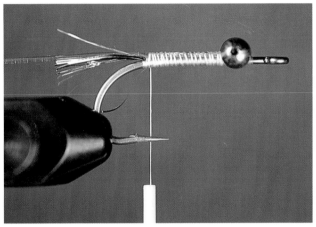

2) Move thread to rear, tie in short, sparse Flashabou tail (Flashabou handles better if moistened) trim excess. Tie in V-rib (laid along hook shank) by wrapping forward, then back again.

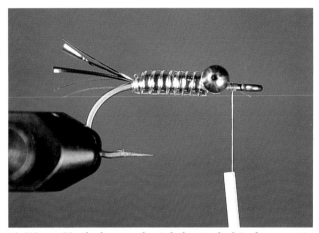

5) Wrap V-rib forward, tightly, to behind eyes, tie down and trim excess. Whip finish to secure thread in front of eyes.

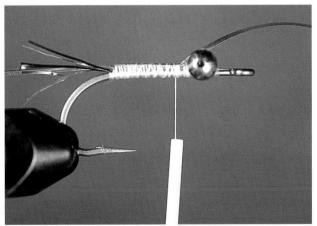

3) Tie in silver tinsel (laid along hook shank) by moving thread to front, behind eyes.

6) Invert hook (if your vise rotates, then rotate). Tie in sparse wing, trim excess (extends just beyond hook). Whip finish and cement.

Del Brown's Crab Fly

Del Brown's Crab Fly—Del Brown

Del first tied his fly in the mid-1980's. He told me, "I realized that it wasn't important to have the exact imitation as much as impressionistic—the idea that it act like a crab rather than look like a crab. And it was immediately effective. We had quite a few patterns that looked pretty good, but the crab would either sink slowly, or else, when it was pulled or stripped, it would elevate. When the crab would elevate, which was unnatural, and the fish would see the boat a lot of times, and turn off.

"My crab would dive to the bottom—the fish would tail up on it and it seemed to work. The whole key to the thing is to have lead eyes, because when a crab sees the fish, the crab frantically dives for the bottom."

Del picked these particular materials for his fly because he says, "I couldn't spin the deer hair. I tried that to make the McCrab and some of those others, and my imitations were so horrible—I'm the world's worst fly tier. I only tie what I can't buy. So Jan Isley came along and said, Well, we're playing around with some yarn. I figured any dummy could cross yarn on a hook, where spinning deer hair took a little more skill. After the fish refused the wild yellow ones that we had, I went to K-Mart and got some natural browns and tans and colors that were similar to the natural crab."

Tying Tips

Del favors chartreuse thread. He says, "I believe in the chartreuse color because there's something magic about that and its attraction for fish."

Hook: Standard; size 2/0 to 4
Thread: Chartreuse flat waxed nylon
Tail (Claws): Mottled cream or brown hen hackle, three per side, splayed out; six strands pearlescent Flashabou
Rubber Legs: White, tips colored with red permanent marker
Body: Alternating bands of tan and brown rug yarn (Aunt Lydia's)
Eyes: Weighted, lead, chrome or nickel plated
Weedguard: Optional

Del says, "Because I'm clumsy, I pre-cut the feathers that I use in the tail, and tie them on one side at a time. The only thing I do different than Dan Blanton or Lefty Kreh is I put the eyes on last.

"After I tie the fly, the last step would be to drizzle on some head cement—I dip the applicator in the head cement bottle and daub it along the hook shank. That helps hold the rubber legs in place. It secures the whole thing." (You can also use Zap-A-Gap super glue.)

Variations

You can substitute rooster hackle for the claws, but hen works better because it's softer and webbier and looks more realistic.

Del says, "While fishing Ascension Bay and some of the places where it's predominantly a white bottom, I tie it with a cream and a tan body (and light colored claws). The crabs are lighter; they take on a protective coloration to match the color of the bottom."

Del has three world records, including a 24 pound permit in the 4-pound test class on his permit fly. He has landed permit up to 32 1/2 pounds and a bonefish of 13 3/4 pounds on his fly.

An important variation is John Kumiski's Fuzzy Crab, which features claws of grizzly hackle tips separated by tan calftail, legs of palmered grizzly hackle, a body of Furry Foam and lead eyes. He ties it to purposely ride hook up (with the lead eyes on top of the hook and the shell of the crab on the underside of the hook). He ties it in brown, cream and olive, catching Florida redfish and black drum (to 30 pounds).

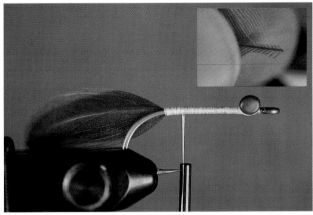

1) Debarb hook, attach thread, cover hook shank. Tie in eyes on top of shank just behind hook eye (leave enough room to whip finish head). Put a drop of Zap-A-Gap super glue on thread to secure eyes. Wrap thread to rear of shank, tie in three hackles that bend to far side (about hook shank length).

1 insert) Leave stubs on stem for more secure thread tie-down.

2) Wrap in three more hackles that bend to near side. Tie in six strands of Flashabou in between claws, 1/2 length of claws. (Flashabou easier to handle when moistened.) (Vise is tipped in photos.)

3) Tie in one strand of dark yarn by criss-crossing thread over it. Tie in one strand of light yarn by criss-crossing thread over it.

4) Repeat until hook shank is covered (with alternating color bands of yarn). Whip finish and cement.

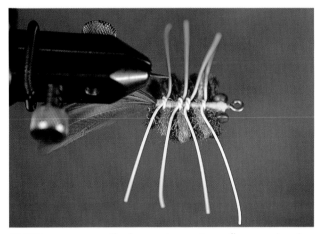

5) Either remove fly from vise or turn fly over in vise (with rotating vise, rotate), trim fly to oval shape. Tie in legs by wiggling them in between yarn strands and tying a square knot in legs. Apply head cement or super glue along hook shank.

6) Trim legs to about hook shank length, with permanent marker, make leg ends red. (Might be easier with fly out of vise.)

Lefty's Deceiver

Lefty's Deceiver—Lefty Kreh

Hook: Standard length; varied sizes
Tail: Three to five pair saddle hackles; six to ten strands Krystal Flash or Flashabou each side
Collar: Bucktail or calftail
Gills: Ten to fifteen strands red Flashabou or Krystal Flash
Topping: Peacock herl or bucktail (medium gray, light green or blue)
Eyes: Optional; painted or adhesive eyes
Weedguard: Optional

This is probably the most famous saltwater fly of all time and still accounts for as many fish as any other pattern in use today. Developed in the late 1950's, the Lefty's Deceiver exhibits all the needed characteristics for an effective baitfish pattern. It has a baitfish shape, is streamlined so it will cast easily without fouling (wrapping around the hook), displays good action in the water and appeals to the fish. Its appeal is further enhanced with painted or adhesive eyes, often the final ingredient that causes fish to strike.

Because almost all saltwater fish feed on smaller fish, you can use the Lefty's Deceiver as a prototype to catch almost any saltwater gamefish, by simply changing the size and coloration to match the prey fish.

Tying Tips

Lefty wrote about tying his fly and the four common mistakes tiers make with the Deceiver in the summer 1990 *American Angler & Fly Tyer*. First, many use neck hackle instead of saddle hackle—saddle works better because it tends to be longer, slimmer, more flexible and curved less than neck hackle. The next mistake is not using enough hackle; a minimum of six (three pair per side) is needed, and on larger flies (size 1/0 and up) four or five pairs should be used.

A third mistake is tying the fly so the hackle flares out, like a swimming frog. Lefty says the Deceiver represents a baitfish, so the saddles on each side are tied so the tips curve inward. Then when the fly is lifted from the water for the backcast it travels through the air like a sleek knife blade.

Lastly, many tiers make the collar too short—the collar should extend beyond the hook bend. The collar forms mini-currents as the fly is retrieved and the "eddies" that roll off that collar move down along the saddles, giving the fly a swimming motion. Just as importantly, the collar prevents the wing from wrapping under the hook while casting.

Lefty offers this advice: "When tying the tail, select three to five saddle hackles that curve to the left when the glossy side is laid down on a table. Select a similar number of saddles that curve in the opposite direction. Lay both sets down so that the butts extend over the table edge. Pick up all the feathers that curve to the left, then pick up those that curve to the right, and carefully put them together so they form a single wing. Make sure the feather tips curve inward. Hold all the feathers between the finger and thumb of one hand, dip the thumb and finger of the other hand in water (from a nearby glass) and stroke the feathers. When wet, the feathers clump together as they should on a finished fly. Using this trick, I tie all the feathers on the hook at one time."

Variations

One reason that the Deceiver is so successful is that it can varied in any number of ways to catch fish all over the world. Lefty wrote, "The Lefty's Deceiver is not really a strict pattern but a method of tying. It can have various shapes, lengths, and colors. The fly can be as short as two inches and longer than a foot for billfish, amberjack, and other species demanding a large offering. It can be tied in a bend-back fashion or with the hook reversed. It has caught everything from striped bass to baramundi to billfish."

1) Debarb hook. Attach thread, tie down tail feathers just in front of hook bend. Cement tie-down area. (See Tying Tips for hackle preparation.) Length varies; try 1 1/2 hook shank length.

4) Invert hook (if vise rotates, then rotate). Tie in 10 to 15 strands red Krystal Flash or Flashabou for gills (shorter than hook point to prevent tangling). Whip finish to secure thread.

2) Tie in Krystal Flash or Flashabou (with uneven ends) along sides of tail.

5) Return hook to normal position. Tie in peacock herl or bucktail (like the darker back of a baitfish).

3) Wrap thread forward to front of hook. (Leave room for collar tie-down and head of fly.) Do collar in two stages: first bunch of hair tied down on far side of hook; second bunch on near side. (No collar on top or underside of hook.) Hair extends beyond hook bend. Whip finish to secure thread.

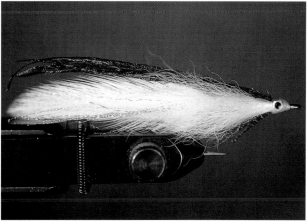

6) Whip finish and cement. Paint on optional eyes or attach adhesive eyes. Protect with fixative or 5-minute epoxy.

Mother of Epoxy (Hot Glue)

Mother of Epoxy

The Mother of Epoxy (MOE) fly has been around for some time now, catching many fish with its simple body formed from weighted eyes covered with epoxy and a tail assembly of hackle, marabou and sparkle materials. Another approach that is quicker and easier is using hot glue. Some of the first hot glue MOE flies used a mold that the tier put the hook and the hot glue into, but that isn't as efficient or as easy as forming the hot glue fly body while holding the fly in your hand.

One advantage of hot glue is that the glue sticks are available in over a dozen colors, including pink, coral, amber, olive and clear. When shopping for a glue gun, make sure it has a smooth trigger and is not the cheap type that require you to use your thumb to feed the glue stick into the gun.

Tying Tips

A hot glue body is easy to make: with the hook in your hand, simply hold the nozzle of the glue gun close to the hook and squeeze little daubs of glue onto the hook. The glue daubs should be about the size of the hook eye. You can kind of push the glue into the form you want with the glue gun nozzle. Once you have the glue on the hook, you can rotate it to prevent sags. The glue will dry in about 30 to 45 seconds. If you get the shape you want, for immediate quick setting and a more translucent look to the glue, dip the fly in water.

If you make a mistake, dip your fingers in water and peel off the glue. If the glue has already set up you can use scissors to cut the glue and then pick it off the body. One of the major advantages of hot glue is that you can re-do a body immediately. And it's cheap—you can do about four dozen size 4 bodies with one stick of glue (and about six dozen for

Hook: Standard, varied sizes (2-8)
Tail: Marabou; hackle; sparkle material; optional craft fur
Hackle: Optional, varied colors
Rubber Legs: Optional, varied colors, round or flat, rubber or silicone (sili legs)
Body: Epoxy (5-minute) or hot glue (varied colors)
Eyes: Weighted (bead chain, lead, non-toxic)
Weedguard: Optional, hard mono

a size 6 hook). So go ahead and make mistakes—I do and it's no big deal. I prefer to make the hot glue body first and then tie on the materials, so I can make a nice body and feel confident about it. (But bear in mind that uneven or imperfect flies still catch fish; presentation is more important than a perfect fly, particularly in saltwater fishing.)

Spread newspapers out under the area where you'll be working with the glue, and since the glue comes out of the gun very hot (mine says its operating temperature is 380 degrees) I recommend that you wear gloves. (When working with silicone, epoxy or hot glue, I wear old clothes and a apron stained from many bouts with dyeing and tying chemicals.)

Variations

For the fly in the photos I used a pink glue stick and pink marabou, grizzly hackle and Krystal Flash (you could use Accent Flash or Flashabou). You can tie the MOE in many color tones, with matching materials; some of the most effective colors are clear over pearl, white, amber, golden yellow, chartreuse, pink, brown, olive, etc. You can vary the fly with rubber or silicone legs, substitute different tail materials such as craft fur or calf tail, and vary the sink rate with different eyes (the glue is neutrally buoyant). You can add one or two strands of stiff monofilament for a weed guard.

You can enhance the glue color by using a similar colored thread, or add light reflection with mylar tinsel or pearlescent sparkle material as an underbody.

Besides the MOE you can make hot glue Crazy Charlies, Big Eye Deceivers, crab flies and other flies where you cover chenille or rabbit fur with hot glue. This hot glue method is versatile, quick, allows the use of various colored glue sticks and is inexpensive.

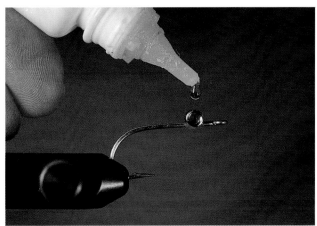

1) Debarb hook, attach thread 1/4 hook shank length behind hook eye, tie in eyes. Whip finish, make sure eyes are level, cement (Zap-A-Gap recommended).

2) Remove fly from vise. Form hot glue body with fly in hand (gloves and working over newspapers recommended).

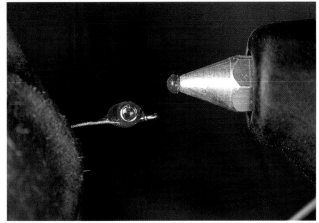

3) Insert fly in vise, attach thread. Tie in marabou (extends hook shank length).

4) Tie in sparkle material along marabou.

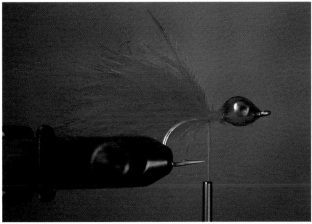

5) Tie in hackle so it splays outward. (Can add another hackle and wrap it around hook shank as collar.)

6) Whip finish, trim thread, cement tie-off.

Siliclone

Siliclone—Bob Popovics

Hook: Standard, size 3/0
Tail: Bucktail; ostrich, sparkle materials optional; saddle hackle, varied colors
Body: Sheep wool, varied colors; silicone; glitter optional
Eyes: Adhesive prismatic

You might think of this fly as having two compartments: the rear is the action section, with bucktail keeping the hackles separated as they undulate during the retrieve; the front is the body, the predator's meal, with the bulk provided by wool impregnated with silicone, which adds form and toughens the body to withstand toothy fish.

Bob Popovics ties the Siliclone and adds a lip to the Siliclone to create the Pop-Lips in his video, "Pop Fleyes" (which I highly recommend that you view). As with the Surf Candy (also in his video), the Siliclone is a kinetic fly, in that part of its construction is movement—applying silicone to the wool. It's really simple to do, and there really isn't any wrong way to do it (other than maybe globbing on excessive amounts of silicone). The Siliclone is typical of flies developed by Bob: they are simple to tie, durable, cast without fouling and they catch fish.

Tying Tips

Saddle hackles for the tail are tied in one at a time, distributed around the shank, on the top, bottom and sides, for maximum action in the water. Before you tie in the wool, use a dog grooming brush on the fleece, which fluffs it up and takes out any tangles or loose hair. (Bob likes the fleece from Rocky Mountain Dubbing Co.)

The first batch of fleece acts as a veil over the forward part of the tail; the silicone on the fleece keeps it from wrapping around the hook (fouling the hook). This first batch is tied in with the tapered ends towards the tail. Later batches are tied in with the butt ends towards the tail, with the tapered ends cut off. The fleece is not spun around the hook; you slide the clump of wool over the shank (centered on the shank), then just tie it down.

You can use almost any clear silicone; Bob recommends GE Silicone II because it has no odor and is easy to find. Bob says he puts on the first coat, working it into the wool "as if I'm trying to dry my finger off". When you smooth the silicone on the second coat, keep it from sticking to your fingers with Kodak Photo-Flo, which is a wetting agent found at camera stores.

When working with silicone, keep paper towels handy. Bob works with the fly in his vise. I recommend working away from your vise, in an area covered with newspapers and away from children and jumping cats or tall dogs with long noses. When working with silicone I wear inexpensive disposable gloves, which allow good tactile feel but keep the silicone off my hands, and then I just discard the gloves after use. (When working with silicone, epoxy or hot glue, I wear old clothes and an apron stained from many bouts with dyeing and tying chemicals.)

To accommodate the curvature of the body, before Bob puts on the adhesive eyes, he first bends the eyes in the middle while they are still on their sheet. He then transfers the eye to the fly with a bodkin. The pre-bent eyes conform better to the body and they stick more securely.

Variations

The Siliclone is a design prototype—you can vary the tail with ostrich or flash materials, and you can vary the size and coloration to match prevalent baitfish, tying the fly in gray, olive or white. Or you can tie your Siliclone in black, chartreuse, red or yellow as an attractor, particularly if you fish turbid waters. With a large eye set closer to the rear, the Siliclone simulates a squid, and calamari are prime food for many gamefish.

As the name suggests, the Pop-Lips fly includes a silicone enhanced wool fleece lip at the front of the fly. When retrieved, the lip causes the fly to wiggle from side to side, a movement that predator fish find hard to resist.

1) Debarb hook, attach thread, tie in bucktail at rear (length about two hook shanks).

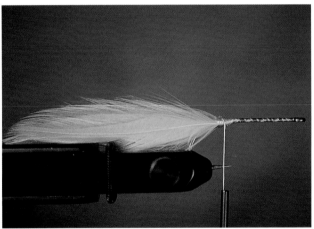

2) Tie in hackle, distributed around hook (length same as bucktail).

3) Tie in small batch of wool, tapered ends to rear (extend back hook shank length), to encircle tail as a light veil. Wool tied down in center, front part trimmed off.

4) Tie in additional bigger batches of wool, butts to rear, with tapered ends cut off. (Shove center of wool clump over hook shank.) Navigate thread through wool to tie it down in center, then again to move thread in front of tied-down clump of wool. Repeat until wool covers shank up to hook eye. Whip finish, cut thread and cement tie-down.

5) Remove fly from vise, fluff out wool with bodkin, trim fly to cone shape, allowing for good hook gap. (Long scissors are helpful.) Apply silicone with finger, pushing silicone into wool, stroking to rear (light coat on wool veil on tail).

6) Bend adhesive eyes while on sheet, attach to fly (with bodkin). Put one dollop of silicone on each eye, on top and on bottom. Put Photo-Flo on finger so silicone doesn't stick, pat down fresh silicone, smoothing out fly.

Surf Candy

Surf Candy—Bob Popovics

Hook: Tiemco 800S, size 1/0
Thread: Clear fine monofilament or white flat
  waxed nylon
Tail: Synthetic hair, white; silver Flashabou or Fire
  Fly; synthetic hair, green, gray, yellow or blue
Body: Silver mylar tinsel or tubing
Eyes: Adhesive prismatic
Gill Slit: Red permanent marker
Overbody: Devcon 5-minute epoxy

The Bob Popovics video "Pop Fleyes" is highly recommended; one of the flies he ties is a Surf Candy, where he shows the tying steps, gives some tips about handling epoxy and shaping the fly, and shows some variations.

An epoxy fly is what I call a kinetic fly, which includes the movements of mixing, applying and fine tuning the epoxy as part of the fly. The advantage of a video is that you can see and hear Bob as he ties the epoxy fly, step by step. The advantage of this book is that when you want to tie the fly, you don't have to use a TV and VCR to fast-forward and freeze-frame to go from step to step. Book photos can't show the kinetic aspect of the fly, but they do lay the fly out on one page.

Although epoxy over synthetic hair adds a dimension of translucency, the greatest advantage to an epoxy fly is durability. It will hold together during casting, but is especially durable when assailed by sharp fish teeth. For really toothy fish, epoxy is tough stuff. (Bob applies epoxy past the hook shank, which keeps the tail material from fouling—wrapping around the hook shank.)

Tying Tips

In the video Bob uses a rotating vise while applying epoxy, and it seems to work well with his setup. He mentions that in his early days he started out by applying epoxy to the fly while holding it in his hand, which is what I prefer to do (thus eliminating the chance of epoxying my vise shut or other disasters). The fly is in the vise in the photos, but I epoxied the fly while holding it in my hand. When the epoxy becomes somewhat firm, I transfer the fly to a fly-drying rotating tool to finish drying. (Set the fly at an angle, not even, to prevent epoxy bulges in the middle of the fly.)

Bob ties all his epoxy flies with two coats of epoxy. He mixes his epoxy on a Post-it because the adhesive strip will keep the paper from moving around; I mix epoxy on discarded can lids and lay newspaper under the working area; however, you can use whatever you want. Bob uses a heavy duty bobkin; I like jumbo wooden toothpicks (Forster "Craft Picks", 750 for less than $3.00) found in the crafts department.

Thoroughly mix the epoxy for about 45 seconds, then apply it to the fly. You set the shape or silhouette of the fly with the first coat of epoxy—while the epoxy is flexible you have control; once it starts to stiffen you should have the shape that you want already set. The second coat is a finish coat to make the fly surface smooth. (Bob will tie a bunch of bodies, then epoxy them.)

Variations

Earlier versions of the Surf Candy featured mylar tubing encasing a trimmed feather to simulate a tail and the lateral line. Now Bob covers the hook shank with a silver material such as mylar tinsel or tubing, then incorporates a stripe of silver sparkle material in the tail, such as silver Flashabou or Fly Flash, extending it to the rear an additional 1 1/2 inches, as inspired by Dan Blanton's Flashtail.

The Surf Candy shown here is an excellent simulation of a baitfish, but it's also a prototype that you can modify to mimic many prey fish. You can vary the coloration, such as going with a light blue back or more of a bright attractor with vivid chartreuse. However, you can also vary the silhouette, from a long slim baitfish to a wide but slender prey fish, while still using the same approach of synthetic hair and epoxy. You can construct a fly that is thin and light enough to cast well, but bulky and imitative enough to trigger a strike from a gamefish.

Some of Bob's variations include the Rabbit Candy, Sea Candy, Squid Candy, Epoxy Sand Eel, Schoolie Fly, Keel Eel and Spread Fly.

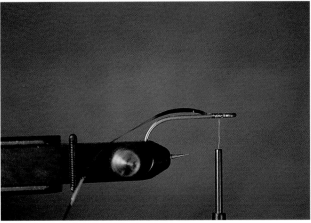

1) Debarb hook, attach thread at eye. Tie in mylar tinsel.

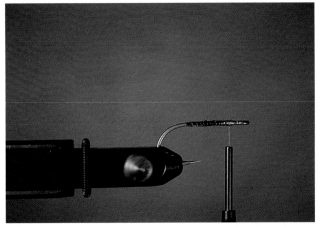

2) Wrap tinsel to rear, then over-wrap back to front, tie off and trim.

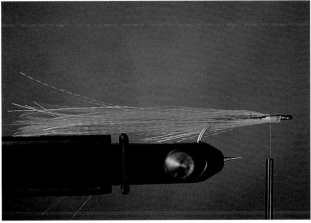

3) Tie in white synthetic hair on top of hook behind eye (extend back about two hook shank lengths). Loosen thread, with fingers rotate hair to distribute around shank, tighten thread. Trim excess.

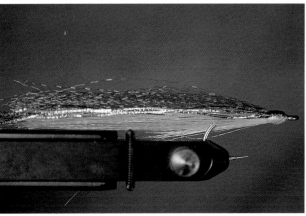

4) Tie in 10 strands silver sparkle material on top, to extend back one inch past hair (moisten to handle easier). Tie in colored hair, trim excess, whip finish and cement. (Keep silver stuff and then darker hair on top—don't rotate around shank.)

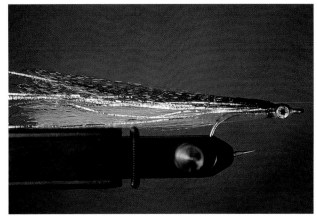

5) Remove fly from vise or use rotating vise. Mix small batch epoxy, apply to fly from eye to just past hook shank, working epoxy into materials. (First coat is a light one.) Keep tail parallel with hook shank. Allow epoxy to dry. Fold eye in middle while still on sheet, remove and attach eye to fly. Make gill slit with red permanent marker.

6) Mix second batch of epoxy, apply to fly body from behind hook eye to just past shank. Until epoxy sets up, keep it evenly distributed.

Tim's Deep Fried Prawn

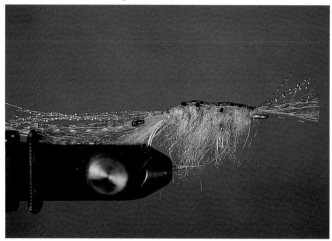

Tim's Deep Fried Prawn—Tim Tollet

The bodies on most saltwater flies are either a material that is wrapped, such as yarn or chenille, or a tubing material such as woven braid. Dubbing is commonly used for shrimp flies because it imparts that illusive illusion of life: the spikes and spicules of the fibers in the dubbing simulate legs, mouthparts, antennae, and other shrimp-like appendages.

Like many aquatic creatures, shrimp may have an overall coloration such as olive or pink that mimics the surrounding vegetation or coral, but to better merge into their surroundings they actually exhibit a blending of colors. For example, a pink shrimp will have some brown and tan in its coloration. By blending different colors in a dubbing mixture, such as cream and olive, you can impart an overall color tone of light olive. The Deep Fried Prawn uses rabbit fur mixed with the complementary color of Lite Brite, which adds bits of lifelike sparkle.

Tying Tips

You'll need to make the eyes ahead of time to allow the black paint or nail polish to dry. To make the eyes, burn the end of the monofilament to form a ball, then paint it black. Cut the mono to about 3/4 inch, then allowing for the eyes to extend to the rear about 3/8 inch, flatten the remainder of the mono with pliers. That allows for a flat surface to tie the eye stalk against the hook shank.

The fly is started down a bit on the bend of the hook, with a bit of rabbit to simulate mouth parts of the shrimp, but also to keep the monofilament eye stalks separated. As

Hook: Standard length; sizes 1 to 8
Tail: Body dubbing; synthetic hair, clear and matches body color; pearl Krystal Flash
Eyes: 50 to 80 pound mono, burned, painted black
Overbody: Plastic bag, 1/4 inch Body Stretch or Scudback, clear
Body: Rabbit dubbing, Lite Brite
Rib: 5 to 8 pound clear monofilament
Front Wing: Extension of tail materials
Colors: Light olive, rootbeer (medium brown), sand (cream), coral (pink), dark sand (tannish cream)
Optional: Overbody mottling with permanent marker: black (for olive or rootbeer body); brown (for cream or coral body)
Note: Because shrimp swim backwards, the "tail" is actually the front of the creature, which includes its feelers, antennae, mouthparts, front legs and eyes. The "front wing" is actually its tail.

you'll see in the photos, after you put on a bit of rabbit, then you add 25 to 30 strands of synthetic hair, half of which are clear and half match the body color. Tie in these synthetic strands so they are of varying lengths, not evened up, with the overall length of the "tail" about one and one-half hook shank length. Add ten strands of pearl Krystal Flash, again with uneven ends, extending about half the length of the "tail". Be sure that the tail materials are long enough to extend out in front of the hook eye for the "front wing".

When dubbing, start at the rear, go forward, then back to the rear, then forward again, building a nice fat body. Start with tight wraps, then allow the later wraps to fluff out some, which you can encourage with a needle or bodkin.

Variations

When Tim first tied this fly he used grizzly hackle under the shellback to achieve the mottled effect, but now finds that a few dabs with a permanent marker achieves the same camouflaging result.

There are dozens of saltwater shrimp patterns, mainly because prawn are a main diet staple of many saltwater fish. One of the most important designs is Popovics' Ultra Shrimp, which uses brown hackle wrapped along the body (palmered) instead of dubbing, and an overbody of clear epoxy.

Tim Tollet, owner of Frontier Anglers, offers packaged dubbing mixtures of rabbit and Lite Brite for tying the Deep Fried Prawn (1-800-228-5263).

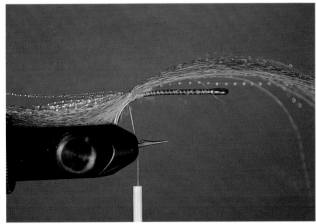

1) Debarb hook, attach thread, tie in tuft of rabbit so it points downward around hook bend slightly (at about 45 degrees). Tie in synthetic hair (clear, then colors that match dubbing) and Krystal Flash; leave rear ends uneven (extend to rear about 1 1/2 hook shank length and a shank length in front of hook).

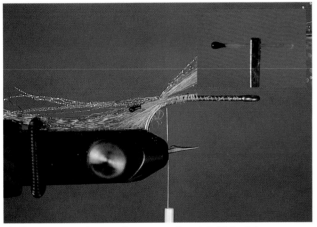

2) Tie in eyes (extend to rear about 3/8 inch).
2 insert) Mono eye stalk about 3/4 inch long, burned and painted black, opposite end flattened.

3) Tie in shellback, then mono for rib. Wax thread, apply dubbing to thread by spinning between thumb and finger.

4) Dub forward to just behind eye.

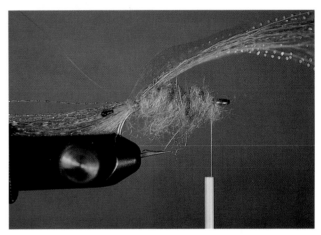

5) Apply more dubbing to thread and dub back and forth over body until a full shape formed, ending behind hook eye (leaving room to tie off).

6) Bring synthetics, Krystal Flash and overbody forward, tie down. Bring mono rib forward (spiral, making segments on body), tie down. Trim front wing to 1/2 hook shank length, whip finish and cement. You can further fluff out dubbing with a needle or bodkin. Add mottling to shellback with blotches by permanent marker.

Whistler

Whistler—Dan Blanton

Dan Blanton of San Jose, California first developed the Whistler series in 1964 for taking stripers in the turbid waters of San Francisco Bay. After 30 years the Whistler design has proven deadly on any fish that feeds on other fish. He wrote about his Whistler in *American Angler*, March 1993 and *The Flyfisher*, Winter 1994.

Dan said, "The Whistler was created to compete with the lead-head, bucktail jig, one of history's top producing artificials. The secret to its huge success is in it's action, the dipping, diving motion that mocks the antics of an injured baitfish—an action that almost instantly pushes a predator's strike buttons. The Whistler has a built-in action that is identical to that of a jig. A bucktail jig gets its action from the mass of lead located at the eye of the hook. This forward heft is what causes the dipping-and-diving action during the retrieve. The Whistler is tied as a weighted fly, concentrating the weight forward in order to achieve the same effect."

Tying Tips

The Whistler derived its name from the whistling sound that bead eyes make on the cast. The bead eyes add more forward placed weight, and the holes in the beads also create underwater sound, further attracting predators.

Dan recommends using crinkly bucktail instead of straight hair. He says, "The crinkly stuff has more action and it takes less of it to provide the same silhouette."

He incorporates two turns of medium red chenille to

Hook: Short shank: Mustad 9175; Eagle Claw 254 Sea Guard; Tiemco 800S; sizes 2/0 to 4/0
Thread: Red Danville flat waxed
Tail: Bucktail; silver Flashabou, 25 to 30 strands; multi-colored Krystal Flash, 15 to 20 strands each side; most have grizzly hackle flanks
Hackle: Three saddle hackles (large and webby)
Body: .030 lead wire (2 amp), 8 to 10 turns; chenille, medium red, 2 turns only
Eyes: Silver bead chain, large

There are over 20 color variations, including all white and all yellow (red bucktail flanks); the rest have grizzly flanks: (bucktail/hackle) white/red, yellow/red, white/white, yellow/yellow, yellow/hot orange, white/bright green, yellow/black, black/black, purple/purple, and others. (The Sunset Flashtail Whistler is pictured: fluorescent red medium chenille; yellow bucktail; yellow or multi-colored Krystal Flash; orange grizzly flanks; two yellow, one hot orange hackle in front.)

simulate pulsing gills, to add to frontal weight and to keep fish from pulling the hackle collar off the fly.

Variations

There are over 20 color variations in the Whistler series, but one important factor to bear in mind when tying this fly is the weight forward design. Dan says, "A properly tied Whistler must be tied on a short shank hook. The first hook I used was an Eagle Claw 318N live bait hook. Today I may utilize the Mustad 9175, Eagle Claw 254 Sea Guard (not stainless), or Tiemco 800S. When using the 254 you must be sure to tie everything from the hook point forward (one-half the hook shank). Utilizing the entire shank of a longer-shanked hook (like Mustad's 3407 or Tiemco's 811S) will negate some of the jigging motion, making the fly far less effective.

"With the exception of hook style changes, I have made only one bonafide improvement to the fly's original design since its inception: the addition of the flash tail, which, in most circumstances, has improved productivity 10-fold, particularly in turbid waters.

"Flashabou and Krystal Flash didn't exist back in 1964 when I began working on the original tie for the Whistler. All my Whistlers are now tied with 25 to 30 strands of silver or other colors of Flashabou buried between layers of bucktail, extending beyond the tail from one to one-and-a-half inches. Krystal Flash is also used liberally in the flanks. The Whistler is an extremely durable fly and if tied properly, one fly should take literally dozens of fish before having to be retired."

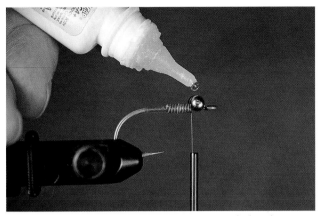

1) Debarb hook, attach thread at rear of shank, wrap forward. Tie in bead chain eyes behind hook eye. Wrap 8 to 10 turns of lead wire behind eyes, wrap thread over wire. Make sure eyes level, spread one drop Zap-A-Gap super glue over tie-down with toothpick.

2) Bring thread to rear of hook. Tie in one bunch of bucktail, tapering stubs. Tie down securely. Tie in 25-30 strands Flashabou on top of bucktail (not on side) extending 1-1/2 inches beyond bucktail, trim excess. (Moisten Flashabou to handle easier.)

3) Add one or two more bunches of bucktail, tie down securely. Tie in 15 to 20 strands Krystal Flash along each side of bucktail, same length as bucktail. Tie in grizzly hackle as flank, not as long as tail.
3 insert) Leave stubs on stem for better thread tie-down.

4) Tie in chenille, make two wraps, tie off and trim excess. Tie in two hackles, shiny side to the front (width about 1 1/2 hook gap).
4 insert) Leave stubs for better tie down, bend stem for easier wrapping of hackle.

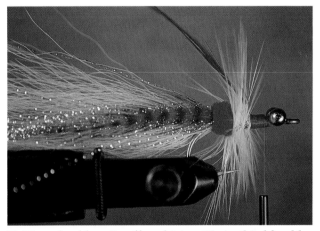

5) Wrap hackles, tie off and trim. Tie in third hackle, same as Step 4.

6) Wrap last hackle, tie off and trim. Wrap thread in front of bead chain, whip finish head and cement. (Option: apply one drop Zap-A-Gap super glue.)

BARBARA MEYER

About the Author

Deke Meyer is a full-time freelancer from Monmouth, Oregon, where he lives with his wife Barbara, who also fly fishes. He tied his first fly from a kit that arrived as a Christmas gift when he was 13 years old. His first size 10 fly had wings more suited for a size 6 fly. But with practice and working on the proper proportions, his flies got better and he caught fish. With the help of this book, and by remembering that fly tying is simply a matter of practice and proportion, you can tie flies that catch fish, too.

His articles have been featured in most of the major fly fishing and outdoor magazines. His previous books include *Float Tube Fly Fishing, Advanced Fly Fishing For Steelhead, Saltwater Flies: Over 700 of the Best*, and the *McKenzie River Journal*.

Previous books in this series include *Tying Trout Flies, 12 of the Best, Tying Trout Nymphs, 12 of the Best*, and *Tying Bass Flies, 12 of the Best* published by Frank Amato Publications. He is currently working on *Advanced Fly Fishing for Largemouth Bass* and *Tying the Top 50 Saltwater Flies*.

If you have any comments or would like to write to the author, he can be reached through the publisher at the following address:

Deke Meyer c/o
Frank Amato Publications, Inc.
PO Box 82112
Portland, OR 97282

FRANK AMATO